the
NEGOTIATOR

the
NEGOTIATOR
a manual for winners

Royce A. Coffin

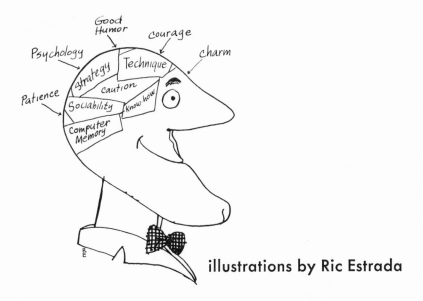

illustrations by Ric Estrada

a division of american management associations

All persons, businesses, and situations shown in this book are entirely fictitious. Any resemblance to any person living or dead or to any existing or previously existing business is coincidental. The author's purpose is only to illustrate certain concepts of negotiating.

International standard book number: 0-8144-5327-9
Library of Congress catalog card number: 73-75768

Eleventh Printing

to patricia,

with whom, after 27 years, I am
still negotiating.

foreword: on winning

"Winning" in a conflict does not have a strictly competi-
tive meaning; it is not winning relative to one's adversary.
It means gaining relative to one's own value system;
and this may be done by bargaining, by mutual accom-
modation, and by the avoidance of mutually damaging
behavior.*

—Thomas C. Schelling

In life generally, and in our business dealings in particular, each of us is required, from time to time, to be a
negotiator. Whether seeking a job, buying a new car or
selling a used home, vying for a promotion, trying to convince management that an outrageous idea is sound, or
attempting to hire a highly talented engineer or sales
manager who has sixteen other interesting offers, you are
(or should be) as deeply involved in the art of negotiation

* The Strategy of Conflict (Cambridge, Mass.: Harvard University Press, 1960).

as the so-called professionals who spend most or all of their time arranging corporate mergers and acquisitions, securing financing for new business ventures, participating in labor contract settlements, negotiating construction contracts, trying to secure governmental funds or support for some industry, enterprise, or project, or, for that matter, running for public office.

In any of these transactions, your ultimate success will depend upon three distinct, if interrelated, factors:

1. A compelling desire to win. Note that, in the sense described by Thomas Schelling in the quotation above, your "winning" is not necessarily, or even desirably, contingent upon someone else's "losing." Indeed, it is the very hallmark of successful negotiations that *both* sides emerge as winners.

2. An understanding of the basic concepts and techniques of negotiation. Although some people are credited with a "natural talent" or "instinct" for negotiating, all the evidence suggests that such individuals have in fact—whether consciously or unconsciously—acquired that talent through observation of, or participation in, a number of transactions with skilled negotiators.

3. A certain amount of iuck. Neither you nor I nor anyone else can do very much to improve our luck; certainly no book can do it for us. What we *can* do, however, is to minimize the importance of luck in our business and personal dealings by learning at least as much as the other fellow knows about the art of negotiating. "Fortune favors the prepared mind."

☐ ☐ ☐

This book is designed to be helpful to those who want to win more often than they lose in business transactions and other negotiating situations. It is based upon my own experience in various kinds of business negotiations, from finding a more challenging and satisfying position for myself to arranging mutually beneficial mergers. In the course of this experience, which has kept me bouncing around the globe for close to thirty years, I learned very early that in most negotiations *success or failure is determined more by the actions, inactions, habits, idiosyncrasies, blunders, insights, and clever strategic moves of the individuals involved than by the terms of the agreement or other formal elements of the proposed transaction.*

As I became more aware of the need for expertise in the conduct of successful negotiations, I decided to document my experiences and observations for my own education, and to develop basic concepts and strategies to review in preparing for each new negotiating session. I did this in the form of simple rules and reminders, illustrated by stick-figure drawings, which I eventually assembled into a homemade, looseleaf manual for reference during my seemingly endless flights from one negotiating session to another. These common-sense guides were based not only upon the many successful strategies and maneuvers that I used or saw others use but also upon the many foolish mistakes that I made or saw others make.

The next logical step, obviously, was to share all this valuable experience with you. Surely out of the several hundred sheets of notes and stick-figure drawings I had assembled I could easily put together a volume of some 400 or 500 pages of practical wisdom and pungent philosophy—*How to Succeed in Mergers and Practically Everything Else*—with 412 footnotes, a comprehensive bibliography, and an extensive index from A ("adding machines, how to conceal") to Z ("zoanthropy, how to deter"). But I recognized that for the busy person there is so much to read that sometimes hands go up in utter despair and only a fraction of what perhaps should be read actually is. And so I asked, Why conform? Why not a book written so that it could be read quickly and reviewed often but which covered the necessary message in an entertaining manner?

Fortunately, I happened upon a wise publisher who agreed with me that the best and most useful thing I could do would be to reproduce these rules and reminders in as brief, simple, and entertaining a manner as possible. Even more fortunately, I found in Ric Estrada a collaborator who not only transformed my clumsy stick-figure drawings into entertaining cartoons but who also contributed substantially to the organization and content of the book—to the point where it is often difficult for either of us to say exactly who contributed what to whom. But that, after all, is the sign (and perhaps the test) of a successful negotiation.

acknowledgments

Hundreds of people have contributed to the experiences that brought about the writing of this book. Recognizing that all who have contributed cannot be acknowledged, I limit my expressions of special appreciation to those *most* involved.

My thanks to the many clients and associates of Arthur Young & Company, Helmerich & Payne, Inc., and Economics Laboratory, Inc., for the opportunity to have the experiences on which this book is based. In particular, I have been greatly helped by Stanley P. Porter of Arthur Young & Company, E. B. Osborn of Economics Laboratory, Walter H. Helmerich III and W. R. Horkey of Helmerich & Payne, and Dr. Robert Wm. Haigh, now with Xerox Corporation.

My thanks, too, to Virgil Wenger of Arthur Young & Company and to Patricia for their encouragement and direct contributions to the book. A special thanks to Al Newgarden of Arthur Young for his many outstanding contributions. And at the risk of repeating myself, let me express again my great appreciation for the creative collaboration of Ric Estrada who contributed much more to this book than he will readily claim or I will readily confess.

And lastly, my thanks to Chris and Patty for their interest and enthusiasm.

Royce A. Coffin

contents

Foreword: On Winning

1 Basic Concepts   1

2 Strategy   23

3 Tactics   43

4 Disciplines   63

5 Analysis   85

6 Psychology   105

7 Details   125

8 Beware   141

9 The Last Word   159

1 basic concepts

This introductory chapter presents a number of basic
concepts which should be second nature to anyone
involved in negotiations. These concepts are essentially
philosophical in nature, as distinguished from the practical guidelines described elsewhere in this book.

1

Enter each negotiation confident that you will succeed, and always remain calm and collected. Never lose your temper. Develop a poker face to conceal your emotions, and never relax or become complacent.

Remember that you must continually sell yourself, your program, or your idea. If your terms are reasonable, your chances of success are excellent. Don't oversell and get in over your head. In discussing terms, start high and *trade down* to your objectives.

Take your time on the more important decisions. Represent yourself and negotiate terms only with principals —never with an intermediary. Don't underestimate others, and remember that successful negotiations are those in which the needs of *all* parties are met.

Never convey a feeling of superiority. Be appropriately humble, but remember that overdoing the humble bit can be dangerous. Stick to your objectives and lose the deal rather than "stretch" and be sorry later.

Regardless of the outcome, you can gain from every negotiaton. Be sure to end each meeting on a positive note and express appreciation to the appropriate people.

Negotiate only with those in authority. Avoid discussing terms with intermediaries whose assignment is to get as many concessions from you as possible before their principals arrive on the scene.

3

Satisfy the needs of *all* parties. *That* is the key to successful negotiations.

Be prepared to trade. Negotiations usually involve a series of compromises. Follow the practice of most negotiators and start above your objectives.

Be calm. Maintaining your cool at all times gives you an unquestionable advantage. Never lose your temper! (At least don't show it.)

Sell. Successful negotiations are primarily the result of your selling yourself and your objectives to others. You get a raise because your boss is *sold* on you. . . . You acquire a company because they are *sold* on you. You get your way through selling.

Don't compromise your objectives. Don't settle in the heat of negotiations for terms which you may later decide are unacceptable. Be prepared to lose the deal if you are not completely satisfied with the terms.

Deal from strength. The successful negotiator deals most effectively when he has identified his strongest points and uses them strategically.

Tell your story yourself. Most situations call for the presentation of information, both written and oral. You should be present to make sure your message is getting across and to learn what you can from observing people's reactions.

Sleep on it. If you have any doubts about a proposal or certain terms, delay your decision until tomorrow. Do not yield to pressures for an immediate decision, which is usually unnecessary anyway.

11

Don't oversell. Overselling—to accomplish short-term objectives—is one of the biggest temptations in negotiations. Whether you're trying to get a job, sell a product, negotiate a contract (wage or other), or convince a company to merge with you, any temporary successes in negotiation may be offset by subsequent failures—losing long-term objectives.

Keep a poker face. Never act pleased as terms
are agreed upon. Be positive, but keep your
tone matter of fact and "as expected."

13

Don't underestimate others. They are strong enough to be in the position of dealing with you.

Be personal. Before or at the beginning of any meeting learn the names of all participants and use them frequently.

Don't be too exclusive. Be sure the other side feels free to include whomever they choose.

Respect confidentiality. The other side may not want employees or others to know that you met or that the subject is under discussion.

Be confident. Enter each negotiation with all the self-confidence you can muster.

Never let your guard down. Three hours of masterful negotiations can be lost in a few minutes of relaxation. The other side may have been waiting for such an opportunity.

Be reasonable. Most people are fair and unless your terms are out of line, you have an excellent chance of succeeding.

Always end on a positive note. Regardless of the outcome, every negotiation has value to everyone involved. Most situations call for an expression of appreciation—know where it is deserved and give it freely.

2 strategy

Here are some guidelines for developing an effective strategic approach to most negotiation situations. These strategies will influence the tone and direction of each negotiation session.

Establish yourself as the leader by taking command of the meeting and gaining the seat at the head of the table. Go more than halfway to meet the other side, and develop a positive theme for the meeting.

Control the number of people in attendance and try to avoid holding meetings in public. Have a total plan in mind so that you can evaluate your progress as you give and take. Make an early concession to get things off on the right foot.

Don't waste your own and other people's time. If a series of meetings is involved, remember that each meeting is a new ball game. Try to identify the needs and interests of others, and adjust your strategy accordingly as the meeting progresses.

Be careful about making work assignments. Avoid asking for information so complex that making this deal won't seem worth the trouble.

Make all offers specific and avoid generalizations or ranges in discussing terms. Don't worry about the end result of your negotiations—if you've played your cards well, you'll win the game.

Sit at the "Head of the Table" in meetings.
Be sure you (or your *chief* negotiator) secure the
No. 1 seat—"end of the table, back to the
window, and facing the door."

Take command of each meeting. Handle
introductions, direct seating, suggest lunch plans,
and be the first to get down to business.

Have a total plan. Without one, most negotiations fail. With your plan and objectives clearly in mind, you can consider the effect of each change as you compromise.

Carefully consider the effect of meetings in public. Be sure that general awareness of your meeting cannot in any way jeopardize its success.

The fewer the participants, the earlier the agreement. In all meetings, keep the number to a minimum. . . . You'll go home much earlier.

Whenever possible, phrase questions for a positive answer. It is a good maneuver to get others in the habit of saying yes.

Be flexible. A minor compromise may pave the way to winning a major point later.

Go more than halfway. If you are the one initiating the meeting, direct all efforts to the convenience of the other side and set the right tone for a successful negotiation.

Make an early concession. Early in negotiations try to satisfy the other side on an area very important to him. He will usually reciprocate on areas important to you.

Don't wait to spill bad news. Most people hate surprises. If something unfavorable develops during negotiations, bring it up on a timely basis. If it has to be told, delaying only weakens your position.

Defer discussions of key issues. Allow enough time to learn all the facts and to fully evaluate the situation and the people involved. You may have to change strategy or even objectives, and it's best to know it before you have gone out on a limb.

Each day is a new ball game. When negotiations take several meetings, don't be surprised if areas previously agreed upon are to be retraded. There has been time to sleep on it and people repeatedly change their minds.

Know the needs of the other side. As quickly as possible discover their *true* needs—usually not what they say they are or buried in a long list. Revise your plans and strategy accordingly.

Make promises with caution. It's easy, in the course of a series of meetings, to say you'll do something, and it's just as easy to be unable to fulfill it.

Don't waste people's time—including your own.
Identify each person's timetable and try to
operate within it. You'll find them appreciative
and cooperative.

Don't keep worrying about the end result. If you concentrate on your plan and handle yourself well, the end result will usually be the right one.

Don't work others. A quick way to bring any meeting to an end is to suggest work for someone else.

Make all terms specific. Never suggest a range of values—the other side will automatically assume that you agree to the lesser value.

3 tactics

We all develop certain techniques or tactics to respond to specific challenges. In negotiating, these tactics have proved reliable and should be used frequently.

Be sure you won't be interrupted—this invariably happens at the worst possible time—and avoid marathon meetings that run on into the wee morning hours. Trying to outlast others is usually a losing game.

Counsel with associates. Learn the value of silence. Avoid (or at least defer) getting into sensitive areas, and take appropriate steps if tempers begin to fray. Keep the meeting rolling along and on the subject.

Be courteous and aggressive, but don't rush the other side. Make it easy for others to agree with you—the path of least resistance is well trodden.

One of the most difficult tactics to master is to be the first to suggest major terms. You shouldn't be negotiating if you don't know your own objectives. Don't be afraid of leaving something on the table. Also, don't be afraid of making too high an offer—it rarely happens. If the other side declares first, they'll think you're trying to beat them down unfairly.

End each meeting on a positive note. When the mission has been accomplished, leave!

Avoid marathon sessions. A tired negotiator makes a poor showing, and you gain nothing by trying to impress people with your staying power.

Be the aggressor. You must take the initiative if you are going to accomplish your objectives. Others will not think or act on your behalf.

Caucus often. Leave the room to counsel with associates whenever you think it will be useful. This eliminates possibly having to retract a statement or point of agreement. The tactic can also be used to relieve tense situations.

Interruptions turn people off. When meeting in your facilities, see that your staff respects your privacy.

Silence is golden. It's the best reply to a totally unacceptable offer.

Be the first to bring up major terms (at the appropriate time). This is one of the most difficult maneuvers for any negotiator to master. Don't be afraid of "leaving something on the table." You shouldn't be in negotiations if you don't know the values involved.

Break the tension. If you get the feeling that people are tightening up, inject humor or suggest a break.

Defer discussion about sensitive points. If you
sense concern on certain areas, try to agree
on as many other terms as possible rather
than risk an early confrontation.

Don't end a meeting on a negative note. If you do, it could be the one thing to stick in someone's mind. After he has slept on it, he just might change his mind about the deal.

Get agreement on next steps. If additional meetings are necessary, don't leave until you set a specific time and place for the next session.

Make it easy. The easier it is for others to do something or to agree with you, the quicker and more positive their response.

Disagree on a positive note. Instead of pointing out where others are wrong, stress the advantages to be gained.

Be courteous. Observing the common rules of courtesy adds greatly to your effectiveness.

Keep the meeting on the track. Be alert for the guy who continually changes the subject. Keep your objective in mind and the meeting on the subject.

Don't react too unfavorably to your own mistakes. Life is one big negotiation, and if you are human, you will make mistakes. Try to keep them to a minimum.

Don't rush the other side. This may be one of the most important decisions of a man's career, and he needs time.

When the mission is accomplished—leave!
This maneuver reduces the chance that someone
will change his mind or that you will continue
to talk needlessly until you finally say the
wrong thing.

4 disciplines

REMEMBER
TO
REMEMBER
TO
REMEMBER...

THINGS TO REMEMBER

Some aspects of negotiation don't come to us easily and usually aren't part of our basic nature. This consideration, combined with a natural tendency to be a bit lazy when it comes to thinking, accentuates the need to review regularly the disciplines described in the following pages.

Never relax is a discipline to be followed at all times in negotiations. Every time you relax you lose ground.

Don't plan on renegotiating at a later date. Stay with your commitments. Avoid the tendency to be an individual star; be a team member and avoid saying the wrong thing. Also avoid the temptation to blow your own horn.

Concentrate on the subject at hand. Try not to rush through the meeting, be punctual and concise, say exactly what you mean, consider the personalities and ambitions of others, and above all be organized.

Years of experience in hundreds of negotiating situations confirm that drinking at the wrong time is one of the most common reasons for *un*successful negotiations. There's a time and a place, and this isn't it.

Don't retrade. Trying to change the terms of the agreement at closing will seriously threaten an otherwise successful negotiation.

Be a team member. When a group is working together in negotiations it is imperative that each participant forgo pride of authorship and follow the plan. Track stars hurt more than they help.

Don't drink. You can't be at your best, and now is not the time to let down.

Be right the first time. If you're not sure, delay answering. Correcting previous statements greatly weakens your position.

Don't slouch. It conveys insincerity and lack of respect. Feet on the table or desk is a real no-no.

Don't be in a hurry. You can't negotiate at your best and you'll probably forget something.

Don't brag. If your personal abilities and achievements must be told, let an associate tell your story.

Concentrate. When others are talking, keep your eyes on them and listen.

Tell it like it is. The other side probably knows all about you and your company and what can be expected from you. Misrepresentations greatly reduce your credibility.

Don't be a nitpicker. Concentrate on satisfactorily negotiating your principal terms and don't jeopardize overall success with possible confrontations on trivia.

Be on time. If you're unavoidably delayed, call and let people know. Unexplained lateness starts negotiations off on the wrong foot.

Say what you mean. Lack of clarity is one of the greatest stumbling blocks to success.

Be organized. Know what you have and where you have it.

Be well groomed. Your confidence will be at
its peak and others will be aware of your
bearing. Carelessness about yourself implies
carelessness about other things.

Don't appear up-tight. Failing to eat or poking at your food while everyone else is enjoying his meal tells the other side how nervous you are.

Think ahead.

Avoid smoke signals. Don't convey nervousness by smoking too much, particularly during discussions on critical points. Maybe now is the time to try that pipe.

"When in Rome, do as the Romans do." There are good reasons for this advice—follow it.

Never say "I told you so." If you've been
proved right, keep it to yourself. You know,
and so will others.

5 analysis

This section might more appropriately be called "Thinking on Your Feet." Entering negotiations well organized and with a plan is a must, but it is equally important to recognize the need, when it occurs, to change your plan completely.

During meetings, be alert for signs that may call for a change in plans or a shift in emphasis. Analyze others closely to note any reluctance or caution they may exhibit during negotiations. Be sure they are listening and "with it."

Study the chemistry among the separate people involved; if the negotiations are to be successful, it *must* be right. This is probably the one most important factor in successful negotiations, particularly where there is to be a continuing relationship after the negotiations are concluded.

You must be there *yourself* if you expect to achieve your goals. Only *you* can change signals to meet your needs and objectives, and how will you judge the need for such change if you aren't there?

Analyze, observe, and don't act hastily. Alert, insightful thinking, combined with the right amount of flexibility, can carry you to success.

Represent yourself. Don't send a John Alden to speak for you. Only you can tell your story with sincerity and convey genuine interest. This may mean more trips than you want to make, but anything worth doing is worth doing right.

Be sure the chemistry is right. If people do not relate well to each other, negotiations will probably eventually fail.

Eyeball to eyeball—discuss terms only in person.
Seeing reactions is a prime key to success.
Discussing terms on the phone or by letter
should be avoided.

Listen! You're heard this one before. You cannot afford to miss anything that's being said. It doesn't hurt every once in a while to tell yourself to shut up.

Spot their leader. In a group meeting, determine who really has authority; he may not be the spokesman.

Analyze office decor. When meeting in others' facilities, observe the surroundings. You'll gain some added insights.

A negative statement may be a "go" signal.
If the other side brings up a reason for not
doing something, they may in reality be asking
you for a solution. . . .

Don't be too critical. Rarely do you have all the facts. Learn as much as you can and reserve judgment. A hasty reaction may cause you to walk away from a good deal.

Evaluate others' success—don't be snowed by their accomplishments. Their success may be due to many factors beyond their control and could only happen once.

Be wary of ignorance. If others are not fully
informed about their areas of responsibility,
adjust your plans as required.

Observe associates. Those around a person, particularly his employees, are a good source for insights.

Look for ways to verify what you are told.
Most information discussed during negotiations
is not supported by facts, but there are many
ways to evaluate statements.

Is he with you? The preoccupied person is not absorbing your comments and is displaying a trait that will give you problems in the future.

Reconnaissance is valuable. Be there early
enough to look the situation over and evaluate.

The early bird gets the worm. At least his composure is a strong advantage.

Reluctance means problems or weakness.
Whenever they keep changing the subject or
avoiding the issue, you know to pursue until
you've got the answer.

Absence is a red flag. Unexplained absences of appropriate key personnel, product data, certain financial information, or "that file I intended to bring" is a strong indicator of weakness.

6 psychology

Most people are a little up-tight at the start of negotiations. The best way to keep things moving in a positive direction is to stay constantly alert to personal sensitivities and to be sure that emotions stay in line.

Avoid any evidence of falseness or insincerity which might threaten your credibility. Be positive in your approach and resist the temptation to discredit competitors or others not present at the meeting. Be careful not to embarrass anyone who is present.

A continuing awareness of each participant and his or her individual mood must be maintained, as moods change constantly. Avoid discussions of immaterial controversial subjects which, if allowed to get out of hand, can keep the meeting from ever getting back to the purpose of the meeting.

Be aware of others' likes and dislikes and plan how to use them to your advantage. Show a genuine interest in others as you begin the meeting (if your interest isn't genuine, you shouldn't be there), and encourage discussion of their personal accomplishments.

Remember that negotiators (like all people) are sensitive. They appreciate understanding and they don't like to be rushed. Take your time and study your opponents.

Be yourself. Putting on an act is soon detected. Others will see through you early in the meeting and you will have lost your credibility.

Don't knock others. Most people don't like to hear criticism. Avoid the temptation to tell how good you are by telling how lousy your competitors are.

Be positive when discussing others' problems.
They will appreciate it, and you'll gain points
by making them comfortable.

Don't embarrass other people. If they make a mistake or thoughtless remark, overlook it and pass on to something else. You'll come out way ahead in every respect.

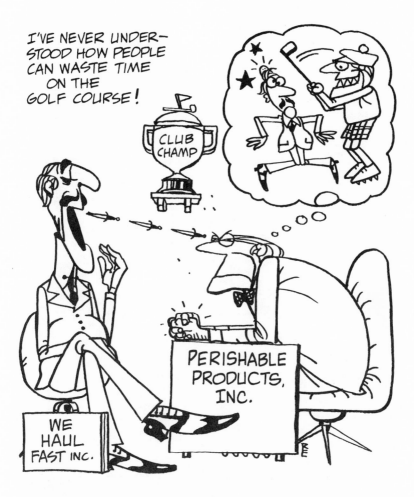

Be cautious about expressing unrelated opinions.
There is no reason for you to expound your
personal theories and opinions. Others probably disagree more often then they agree, and
so you stand to lose more than you gain.

Don't be unpleasant. A belligerent reaction, offensive statement, or a critical remark only adds fuel to the other side's feeling of superiority.

Respect others' personal preferences. If there are no ashtrays, take the hint and refrain from smoking. And don't bang your briefcase on the desk.

Show interest in others. Unless the group is quite large, begin the meeting with a personal comment. A glance around their office— pictures, trophies, paintings—will give you plenty to work from.

Be sensitive to others' moods. Each negotiating situation is different and must be planned separately. Every person is unique, and even moods may vary from day to day.

Be patient. Near the end of the meeting(s) when summarizing or formalizing an agreement, you may find that some points of agreement may have been forgotten. Refer to your notes and be prepared to renegotiate.

Don't push too far. Every negotiator has a breaking point. Be sensitive to the people you are dealing with and don't ask for too much. Greediness has aborted many an otherwise productive meeting.

Expect negative reactions. Regardless of what you offer, the other side probably won't think it is fair.

Think before you speak. Respect personal and
professional tastes of others. Many a successful
negotiation has been nullified by a personal
critical remark.

Be understanding. Let others know you appreciate the compromises or sacrifices they may be forced to make.

Acknowledge others' contributions. They take pride in their abilities and accomplishments. Express your awareness of what they bring to the table.

Respect identity. Recognition is very important to most people—it may be a company name, product identification, pride of authorship, or formal recognition of contributions. Minor concessions reap big returns here.

Show interest. Your interest in others' personal achievements greatly enhances your chances of a successful meeting.

7 details

Let's deal with some of the "little" things that are easily
overlooked but yet weigh heavily on the results of
negotiations.

Begin by selecting your negotiating team carefully. Be sure that each member understands the strategy. Don't include anyone who is not needed, and don't include someone who might violate the ground rules of negotiating.

Set the right tone by furnishing the meeting room properly. Do your homework and keep your proposal simple.

Volunteer for the task of keeping notes. It's easy to avoid responsibility for such documentation, but keep in mind that only *you* know exactly what should be recorded. The last person you want to document the meeting is someone from the other side.

Be sure there's no misunderstanding about each point agreed upon. Avoid having to renegotiate at a later date.

It's a good idea to set a preliminary meeting at the other party's facilities, where they are most likely to be at ease. When it comes time to negotiate, however, be sure you're meeting on your turf.

A mistake often made is to build up the numbers on your negotiating team till you overpower the other side. More than a few negotiators have been scared off by the feeling of being surrounded.

Many small but significant things happen during meetings, and you must stay on top of all that goes on. Be sure that everyone follows through on the promises and commitments he or she makes and that nothing is forgotten.

Be prepared. Never enter a situation unless you have done your homework and are as knowledgeable as possible about the other side.

Document. Keep complete notes on all points of agreement and have them typed and circulated at the close of each meeting. Fastidious record keeping has a way of eliminating any need for renegotiation.

Keep the numbers even. When your plans involve a number of people, see that the other side knows about it. Don't try to overpower them.

Select your team carefully. At the beginning
of a series of meetings, set the right tone by
selecting positive-thinking participants. Keep
technicians out of the room but available
for counsel.

Organize the meeting room ahead of time.
Remove the possibility of digressions to handle
details of arrangements and materials.

Clarify each point of agreement. Don't assume anything—be sure. Repeat the terms if necessary. It's twice as hard to renegotiate later.

Avoid disappearing acts. Many situations call for associations after an agreement has been reached. Be sure the other side knows this isn't the last they will see of you.

Delegate only with control. Quite often in the heat of the moment many persons are assigned certain tasks. Unless you know who has what and when it is to be done, an otherwise successful negotiation may never come to fruition.

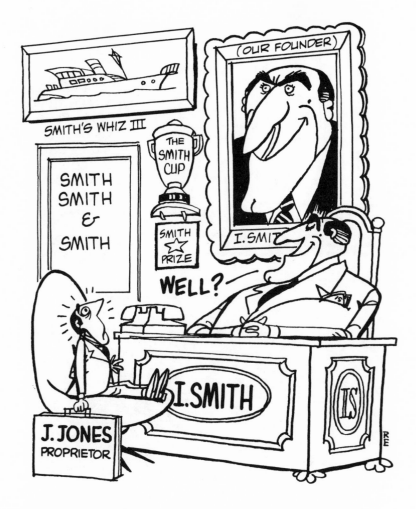

Negotiate in your territory. If your situation offers the choice of where to negotiate, *always* discuss terms at your facilities. The opposite holds true for "getting acquainted" sessions.

Keep it simple. If complexities are unavoidable, at least begin with an easily understood summary. People will never agree to something they don't understand.

Site selection is a critical factor. When choosing a neutral meeting place, secure colorful rooms in pleasant surroundings and avoid drab and oppressive settings.

Breakfast meetings are often disappointing.
Many people find breakfast a bad time to talk
business, particularly at the first meeting. Some
people feel that way about any meal—it is
difficult to make a good impression while eating.

Be a good host. The right mood is set for a successful meeting when you provide for caucuses, private phone calls, paper work, and other amenities.

Timing is a critical factor. Most people are at their best in the morning (10:00 A.M. is the prime time) and this is the time to begin negotiations or initiate contact.

8 beware

It would be nice to think that everyone is above using gimmicks or tricks in negotiating, but over the years I've learned that this isn't always the case. One trick is to arrange the meeting room so as to convey one side's superiority and give it a physical advantage. Insincere flattery and provocative statements are two strategems to throw you off balance.

Make sure about the motives of the people you are dealing with. Are they sincere? I've participated in many meetings in which the other side's sole objective was to learn as much as possible about our company and then to use the information for their own benefit and our detriment. Be cautious of wandering eyes—many a negotiator can read upside down (and sometimes through thin paper). Avoid putting anything on a desk or table unless you expect it to be read.

If you're meeting at the other fellow's place of business and you're not offered comfortable facilities, you can be sure that you're not wanted. This tactic requires close scrutiny on your part.

Be careful about depending on others to report back on unresolved items, particularly if it's an area of dispute. They'll probably "forget," in the hope that you'll do the same.

Don't let yourself be lulled into overconfidence. Watch out for the report that omits basic facts or arranges information so that you don't see the true picture.

Observe office furniture strategy. Many try to imply superiority through its selection and arrangement.

Watch the windows. Another trick is to force
you to look into the sun or at least a strong
glare.

"I'm really a good guy." The next step is to walk
around the desk and sit with you at the time
of decision.

You'll never get the whole story. If the other side has problems or pending trouble, don't expect to be told about it until after your deal has been consummated.

Be wary of the flatterer. Until someone knows you quite well, his flattery usually means insincerity.

Beware of provocation. Many negotiators make wild statements to throw you off balance. Consider your reactions carefully and don't respond until you are sure of what you want to say.

Be alert for strained eyeballs. Assume that all negotiators can read upside down (and through thin paper). Don't leave anything out in view that you wouldn't publish in the local newspaper.

Be cautious when you're not wanted. You know you're not welcome when your surroundings leave something to be desired. Better probe these situations.

Find out what's *really* on their mind. One sneaky maneuver often used is to enter negotiations to learn as much as they can about you and/or your business and then to use it to their advantage (and to your disadvantage).

Look out for the procrastinator. Some negotiators volunteer to check into a touchy situation or get additional data to you. If they drag their feet about it, they are hoping you'll forget.

Be sure you have all the facts. Information may be furnished to you in a manner that implies certain strengths or camouflages certain weaknesses.

Watch out for the faker. Many negotiators smoke too much, act nervous, and go through other physical gyrations trying to make you feel overconfident.

Don't get taken by the pack rat. This character will ask to look at reports you have prepared— and that's the last you'll see of them. (Hang on to your pen and pencil.)

Don't be fooled by the cover. Some reports are heavy on form and light on content. If they're well done, they can hide bad news.

Don't be taken by the soft-soaper. Most of us have a favorite subject, a special weakness. A popular maneuver is to soften you by bringing up the subject early in negotiations.

Watch out for snow jobs. If people are in trouble with you and know they are wrong, they should admit it. But this rarely happens— usually they begin the meeting with long and strong oratory, hoping to wear you down.

9 the last word

Even if you have done everything right, you can still lose
if you don't take one last but critical action—*check the
contract* against your notes of what has been agreed.
This is important to do when you have prepared the
final documents; it is critical when they were prepared
by the other side.

Be absolutely sure there are no surprises in fine print.